T0142537

THE
BIBLE
REVEALED

LILLIE PETERSON

Edited by Alisa St. Amant

WESTBOW
PRESS®
A DIVISION OF THOMAS NELSON
& ZONDERVAN

WestBow Press books may be ordered through booksellers or by contacting:

WestBow Press
A Division of Thomas Nelson & Zondervan
1663 Liberty Drive
Bloomington, IN 47403
www.westbowpress.com
844-714-3454

Scripture taken from the King James Version of the Bible.

ISBN: 978-1-6642-2465-0 (sc)
ISBN: 978-1-6642-2466-7 (e)

Library of Congress Control Number: 2021903308

Print information available on the last page.

WestBow Press rev. date: 03/18/2021

Preface

I wrote this book due to a dream I had a few years ago when I was a Sunday school teacher. During the years I taught Sunday school, parents brought their children to attend my classes, and I observed they did not know the Bible or Jesus Christ. Each time I came in contact with these young people having little or no spiritual knowledge, it bothered me.

One night I had a dream, and in it, I heard, "Feed my children." I pondered about what the dream was trying to convey to me. Suddenly, I started writing this book, and as I wrote, calm filled my soul, I understood my vision.

Note: All Bible verses quoted in this book are from the King James version.

Introduction

The Bible contains the laws that every Christian should live by. God has given us special people to learn how to understand and study the Bible; these people are preachers, teachers, ministers, etc. Everyone that God uses to teach His words should make sure that they learn the Bible; so their teachings are accurate. And also, so they can explain the text God has given them. When someone teaches the Bible, not one word should be changed or added to the scriptures. Everyone should take the time to read the Bible for themselves. This will help you better understand what is being taught, and you will know if what you are being taught is true.

The main purpose of this book is to introduce youth to the Bible and some of the miracles within it. A character named AmaZING was created to assist them as they read this book. This book will help youth understand the Bible better, as it contains numerous scriptures from the Old and New Testament. Its purpose is to capture the interest of children and hopefully encourage them to read the Bible.

"I created a character named AmaZING to help you as you read this book. I believe it will be helpful in two ways: it offers verses to help you along the way and it gives you space for notes in some areas. Maybe you can think of other ways AmaZING can be useful to you."

AmaZING

AmaZING is to be wonderful, or to be surprised. For I feel wonderfully blessed to be of assistance to you and your friends. I will appear on numerous pages Throughout this book, to ask a question or to quote a Bible scripture. So get your Bible; you may want to read it as you discover some amazing facts.

What does the word Bible mean, and what is it about? According to the Merriam-Webster Dictionary, "the Bible is the sacred book for Christians." The Bible is a book of instruction given by God. It is also a book with numerous parables to help anyone in any given situation.

Who is God? God is the Creator of everything, even you and I. The Bible states, "In the beginning, God created the Heavens and the Earth (KJV Genesis 1:1). According to Revelation 1:8,

"I am Alpha and Omega, the beginning and the end, saith the Lord, which is, which was, and which is to come, the Almighty."

The Bible is divided into two parts; the Old and New Testaments. The Old Testament is made up of thirty-nine books. These books tell of how God dealt with the Jewish nation before Jesus Christ was born. It also explains the origin of man. It reveals how God created the Heavens and the Earth, the universe, and even you and me.

The New Testament consists of twenty-seven books. And it contains the life and death of Jesus, our Lord, and Savior; God's only begotten Son. Within it, you can also find out how He lived on Earth as a perfect being. He gave up His life for the sins of man, for God loved us so much that He did not want to destroy the human race.

I did not write this book to take the place of your Bible. I wrote it to introduce you to the Bible and perhaps to encourage you to read the Bible. Yes, I wrote it for believers and non-believers. You should be ready to experience the excitement and sorrows as you journey through the pages of the Bible.

OLD TESTAMENT

AmaZING

My first question is: What is Genesis the beginning of?

Hint — Genesis 1:31; 27

Genesis is the first book of the Bible and the Old Testament. It is called Genesis or The first book of Moses, called Genesis". Genesis should be the beginning; it is the beginning of the world, time, life, sin, and thank God for salvation, the first man and woman, and animals of the wild. It expounds on the creation of everything; and how sin started.

God placed man in a beautiful garden called the Garden of Eden (Gen. 2:8-17). It was a beautiful place filled with fruit trees from which man could eat. Within the garden, Adam and Eve, the first humans, were told not to eat from the tree of knowledge (Gen. 2:9) that stood in the middle of the garden. It seemed when God said don't; it became tempting because they ate from the same tree that God instructed them not to. You will discover the first sin made by man (Gen. 3:1-24). Then learn about the consequences that followed their sinful action.

This book explains how God sent Moses to lead the Israelites out of Egypt, where they were slaves (Genesis 1-19). It closes with the Israelites, a people chose by God, enslaved in Egypt.

AmaZING

There were ten plagues sent upon Egypt by God. Why? And where in Exodus can they be found?

Hint — pages 4-5 of this book

Exodus is the second book of the Bible; it is also called the second book of Moses. Exodus means to leave or exit a place. "And the Lord spake unto Moses and unto Aaron, and gave them a charge unto the children of Israel, and unto Pharaoh king of Egypt, to bring the children of Israel out of the land of Egypt" (Exodus 6:13). God chose Moses and his brother, Aaron, to approach the Pharaoh of Egypt on their behalf. They were to convince the Pharaoh to set the Israelites free. The Pharaoh was mean, and he did not believe in God. He would not listen to Moses pleas for his people's freedom. He made the people work harder, longer hours, gave them small amounts of food. After Pharaoh made it harder for the people, they stopped listening to Moses. So he retreated to God in prayer, and God said, "...See, I have made thee a god to Pharaoh: and Aaron, thy brother, shall be thy prophet" (Exodus 7:1 KJV). He gave them special abilities to do miracles for the Pharaoh, to prove to the Pharaoh, they were sent by God. But he was so mean and stubborn; he thought they were magicians like the ones in his kingdom.

So God used a different strategy, he sent ten plagues on Egypt: blood (7:14-25); frogs (8:1-8); gnats (8:16-19); flies (8:20-30); livestock (9:1-7); boils (9:8-12); hail (9:13-35); hail (9:13-35); locust (10:1-20); darkness (10:21-29; and death of the first born animal and child (11:1-10).

- God turned all the water in Egypt to **blood.**
- The entire land was swarming with **frogs.**
- God allowed the dust or dirt to transform into **gnats** that contaminated all of the lands of Egypt.
- **Flies** invaded every home in Egypt.
- God sent a plague that destroyed all the **livestock** (cows, horses, donkeys, camels, oxen and sheep) in Pharaoh's kingdom.

- He instructed Moses and Aaron to take handfuls of ashes from a furnace, throw them in the air in the presence of the Pharaoh. When they did, everyone in Egypt became infested with **boils**, even the animals.
- Moses warned Pharaoh and his officials of a **hail** storm. Some believed and did as they were told, but Pharaoh and the people that did not believe went on with their daily lives. All of the people and animals that were outside died when the hail came.
- There were so many **locusts** they could not see the ground. The Locusts ate everything in sight, the crops and even the trees.
- Moses was instructed by God to raise his hands towards heaven, which caused darkness to fall upon Egypt for three days. What a scary feeling, having no light of any form for three whole days.
- The last plague God placed upon Egypt was the **death of the first born** child and animal. After all of that occurred, Pharaoh was happy to let the Israelites go free. He rushed them out of Egypt because now he believed in God.

After they gained their freedom, Moses led them to Canaan. God said, "And I have said, I will bring you up out of the affliction of Egypt unto the land of the Canaanites, and the Hittites, and the Amorites, and the Perizzites, and the Hivites, and the Jebusites, unto a land flowing with milk and honey" Exodus 3:17. The Israelites were God's chosen people. He stayed with them throughout the entire journey. He fed them, led them, and protected them, and they were still disobedient, grumbling people.

In the book of Leviticus, it is said that fire fell from Heaven. Did it actually fall? And where can I find it?

Hint – Number 9:24

Leviticus is the third book of the Bible; it is also called the third book of Moses. Within this book, God gave Moses some laws that He wanted the Israelites to live by. The laws are in Leviticus chapter 17 through 27:33. There were rules for the people and the priests. I shall mention some of them: Do not marry a family member; do not take part in homosexuality; do not steal or tell lies; do not curse your parents. You can read all about them yourself in the chapters mentioned above. This book encouraged the Israelites to live godly lives as they traveled through the wilderness.

If you want to live your life according to God's Word, you should commit yourself to these commandments with your whole heart. These laws are there to protect us, teach us how to treat one another, that He is the only God, and about love. The love we should have for God and each other.

AmaZING

Numbers is the fourth book of the Bible; it is also called the fourth book of Moses. In this book, the Israelites are led by Moses to the land promised to them by God. After traveling for two years, God told Moses to take an inventory of all people, separate the Israelites according to their tribes, write the names of all the males that were twenty and above, all that could fight or go to war. God told him to appoint a leader for each clan or tribe. Some more tribes were among the Israelites, so God told Moses to do the same thing with those tribes. After Moses finished his tasks, there were twelve tribes, and he gave each a leader. After the tribes were separated, Moses gave the people instructions from God. A few of the instructions were to assign jobs to certain men, purify the camps of sickness and anyone that touched the dead. The people were so ungrateful, but God loved them and continued to allow Moses to lead them to the land He promised, Canaan. They complained so much that God became furious with them. He sent fire down from heaven, and it destroyed the outer edges of their camp. It was so bad they approached Moses for help. Moses prayed to God, and the fire ceased. The fire destroyed so many people and tents they started calling that land "Taberah." The people would travel for a while and suddenly forget about God's grace and mercy and about the consciences their murmuring had cost them. How can anyone forget about how God was a blessing and delivered them from slavery?

When they arrived at the land God promised to give them, Moses sent the leaders of the twelve tribes out as scouts to evaluate the land and the people that lived there. It took the scouts forty days to return with their report, in which they had one for the people and one for Moses. They told the people what they saw and showed the large over-sized grapes they brought back. Then they told Moses that the land was "flowing with milk and honey" or the land was so rich with food; they even showed him some proof, the grapes. They told Moses, "the people who inhabit Canaan are giants, and the cities are walled up; it will be impossible for us to live there." But Caleb, of Judah's tribe, stood before Moses and the people, trying to convince them to enter the land God had promised. He said, "Let us go up at once, and possess it; for we are well able to overcome it," 13:30. Can't you hear what the people must have said: If they are giants, they will put us back in slavery; surely they will beat or kill us. You know we should take a stand for what we want in life. There are so many times in our lives that we allow fear to rule it. It's like this, I want to drive, but I am afraid I'll have an accident. We, as people, expect God to put it in our hands. We want him to say, take it, you don't even have to leave home. If you want something bad enough, you would be willing to do what it takes to get it.

Deuteronomy is the fifth book of the Bible and is also called the fifth book of Moses. God allowed Moses to see the land that He promised to give to Abraham, Isaac, and Jacob; but he could not enter. You can learn why Moses was only shown the Promised Land and not allowed to enter by reading 20:12 & 35:51.

This book helps the Israelites remember that God is always there for them and helps them remember the promises they made to God. Moses tried very hard to encourage the Israelites to obey the laws that God gave them, but they were stubborn and ungrateful. Have you ever heard the song "No Charge by Shirley Caesar?" It goes something like this; "for the nine months I carried you growing inside of me, there is no charge." I said that to say this, God fulfilled all the promises He made to the Israelites. He stayed by them continually, protecting them, feeding them, and leading them. But despite all God did for them, they would not be obedient to God or His laws. Your inquiring minds should want to know why; since God was leading and feeding the Israelites.

These people begged continuously for the things they received as slaves in Egypt. God made sure their stomachs were full, but they had to have meat. They told Moses, we are sick of manna or bread. In other words, they would rather live in slavery, just for a piece of meat. When we were in Egypt, we ate meat, and we want some now. For their great desires, God sent them some meat. He said it would not be for just one or two days or even twenty. How long do you think God supplied meat for the Israelites? And what happened afterward? To find out what happened after God gave them the meat they so badly desired, read 11:18-20.

How can we forget so quickly all that God does for us? The Bible tells us to be careful as we go about our daily lives, that we don't forget about God, 8:11. We should remember that God is love, which means he loves us unconditionally. And the Bible tells us to love Him with everything we are, that is, with our whole hearts or all that we are. We are to love Him all the time, not just when we think we need Him, for He is there all of the time waiting to hear praises and waiting for your call.

AmaZING

Joshua died at the age of 110 years old. Where did they bury him? Joshua 24:30

Joshua is the sixth book of the Bible; in this book, Joshua was chosen to lead the Israelites or the chosen people after Moses's death (1:1). He was dedicated to God and the people. He worked hard to make sure the people followed the laws that God had given o Moses. He was the Son of Nun, as well as the assistant of Moses. All the events in Joshua took place in the Promised Land of Canaan.

After Moses' death, God said to Joshua, "Moses my servant is dead; now therefore arise, go over this Jordan, thou, and all this people unto the land which I do give to them, even to the children of Israel," (1:2). Gold also told him not to be afraid to do what he was told (6:9); for He said, "I command you—be strong and courageous! Do not be afraid or discouraged. For the Lord your God is with you wherever you go." In other words, I have your back.

Within Joshua's book, God performed numerous miracles. He allowed the sun and the moon to stand still (10:12-14); shouting tore down an entire city, and so on. The Bible teaches us about the good and the bad things that happen within our lives. Miracles are shown to us daily, but we miss many of our blessings since we have little or no faith. If we would slow down and look around, we can see the miracles of God.

Read about the army composed of Angels, protection sent by God to fight numerous enemies that came in contact with the Israelites. They were instructed to stop worshipping idol gods and follow God (24:15). When they decided to follow God, Joshua destroyed all the idols and built an altar for worshipping God (24:24).

AmaZING

Who was Deborah? Judges 4:4, 5

Judges is the seventh book of the Bible; in this book, Joshua died at one hundred and ten years old (2:8). As years passed, the new generation did not know the laws, so they started worshiping Baalim. Judges describes Israelite history during a period of idolatry, sin, evil, rebellion, and repentance. This book records the history of the Jews from Joshua's death to Samuel's birth as they reside in the Promised Land of Canaan. It also shows us that when we fall, we don't have to stay down. We can always return to God. He is willing to accept us back. His arms are still open.

The book of Judges instructs us to watch what we do to others; because God sees everything we do. For example, a king named Adoni-bezek, when his army captured a king, he would have their thumbs and big toes cut off. So, when the Israelites captured him, they cut his thumbs and big toes off (1:4-6). Then there was a woman named Deborah, she was a prophet, and later she became a judge. She also went to war with Baraka and his army. She killed Sisera (4:17-25).

Do you believe that 300 soldiers can kill or defeat 135,000 soldiers? According to Judges 7:1-8:21, that is just what they did as God stood with them. A woman bashed King Abimelech's head in with a stone used to grind grain to make bread (9:50-53). I know that everyone has heard of reading about the strongest man in the world, Samson and that he fell in love with Delilah, a cunning woman. Samson fought with a lion; he tore its head apart by pulling its jaws apart.

In this book, you will also find twelve names of people that judged Israel. They are listed in chapters thirteen through sixteen. But only two of the named judges are talked about more than the other fourteen: Deborah, a woman, and a prophetess; Gideon, a man with very little self-esteem. Even though he was afraid, God chose him to lead the army when they fought the Midianites. God showed him a miracle to encourage him. He told God I need to see more (6:36-40).

AmaZING

| Did Ruth have spiritual ancestors? Ruth 4:16-17 & Matthew 1:5 |

Ruth is the eighth book of the Bible. Ruth was a Moabite woman; she and her people worshipped idol gods. Later in the story, you will see how Ruth became devoted to Naomi, her mother-in-law.

Naomi was married to Elimelech of Judah; they had two sons, Mahlon and Chilion. Elimelech took his wife and sons to Moab because there was a famine in the land of Judah. After being there for a while, Elimelech died. And his sons decided to take Moabite women as wives. Then after a time, both sons died, leaving their wives and their mother, Naomi. After their deaths, Naomi told her daughters-in-law that she was going back to Judah in Bethlem; because she heard that God had blessed that land again. So they gathered their belongings and started on their way to Judah; suddenly, Naomi decided to send her daughters-in-law back to their homeland of Moab. When she told them to go back, Oprah took Naomi's advice and went home to her family and their idol gods; but Ruth decided to stay with Naomi because Naomi was an old lady that needed someone to care for her, and she loved Naomi as a mother. Ruth told Naomi, I am going to stay with you to make sure you are cared for. I will accept your God as my God, and your people shall be my people. Read the story to find out if God accepted Ruth after she abandoned her gods and her people. Naomi was a Hebrew that worshipped the one true God, and Ruth had always worshipped idol gods. But Ruth gave her life to God and cared for Naomi as if she was her mother. Back in those days, it was the duty of a son to take care of his mother; but Naomi's sons were dead. Ruth's loyalty to her mother-in-law and her devotion helped her win the heart of Boaz, a man of wealth. I am sure you will enjoy this remarkable story as you read it for yourself.

AmaZING

Who fought with the giant named Goliath? 1 Samuel 17:41-58

I Samuel & II Samuel are the ninth and tenth books of the Bible. The first book of Samuel contains information about numerous fascinating people. I will introduce you to a few: Elkanah and his wives Peninnah and Hannah; Samuel, the last judge; Saul, the first king of Israel and David, the greatest king of Israel.

Now let's chat about Elkahan and his family. Every year, he would take his family to Shiloh's Temple to worship and give sacrifices to God. Every year while at the Temple, Elkanah's wife, Hannah, prayed to God for a child. His other wife, Peninnah, had two sons, and Hannah did not have any children. So she prayed to God regularly for a child. When Peninnah would see Hannah praying, she made fun of her often, calling her infertile and other names. When Peninnah teased Hannah, it made her sad. How would you feel if someone teased you or called you names?

One day when Hannah was praying in the Temple, Eli, the priest, saw her; as he looked, he could only see her mouth moving; but there was no sound coming from her mouth. So he came to the conclusion that she had been drinking. Sometimes we misjudge a person because of what we see or don't see or hear. Often, we become prejudice because of how a person looks, dresses, their culture, etc. Eli concluded that Hannah had been drinking because she was inaudible. He instructed her to throw the wine away and never come to the Temple drunk again. Hannah told him, I am not drunk. I was talking to God from my heart.

Even though Eli insulted her, she thanked him and returned to her family. Here is an example of Hannah's situation: Once I watched a western, a young cowboy was traveling across the country alone. He felt tired, so he decided to find a place to rest for a spell or a while. He saw a small farm, so he went there to ask the farmer if he could sleep there, but no one was home. So, the cowboy decided to take a nap in the barn. He heard some shooting and woke up. One of the men fired by the farmer had returned to the farm to steal one of the farmer's horses; because his horse was lame. Before he could steal the horse, the farmer returned home, and they started shooting at each other. Just as the cowboy took his gun from its holster, the farmer fell backward into the barn; he saw the cowboy and assumed he was with the man he had fired. So the farmer shot the cowboy. Now back to the story. Hannah's family arose early the next morning to return to Ramah, their homeland. That same night Elkanah and his family made it home, he took Hannah to bed, and she became with child. She later gave birth to a son, which she named Samuel. He grew up serving the Lord (1 Samuel 2:21). Hannah promised to give him back to God if He blessed her with a child. And when he was old enough, she took him to the Temple to work with the priest.

Eli, the priest, when he became an older man, was informed his sons were evil. They were seducing the young ladies that helped at the tabernacle's entrance. They had no respect for God (1 Samuel 2:12) and ate food that the Israelites sacrificed to God for their sins. They even took some of the raw meat because they wanted to roast it for themselves. God became very angry with Eli because of all the terrible things his sons were doing.

AmaZING

Who destroyed the dynasty of Baasha? Why? 1 King 16:11-14

I & II Kings are the eleventh and twelfth books of the Bible, written to show the difference between the people who lived according to God's will and those who refused to acknowledge Him. According to the books of Kings, Solomon was the wisest man in the country where he lived. God abundantly blessed him, and his wisdom exceeded all the other people. He was so good; he wrote 3,000 Proverbs and 1,005 Songs (1 Kings 4:32). God chose him the new king of Israel, and he built a temple for the Ark of the Covenant of the Lord. God Stopped all wars against Israel (1 Kings 5:4), so the people could complete the Temple without interference. Solomon used a lot of money, favors, materials, and unique woods to complete the Temple to the best of his ability. Animals were used as a sacrifice to ensure the building process was pleasing to God. God showed His approval as He filled the Temple with thick dark smoke (1 Kings 8:10-11). Upon finally finishing the Temple, the people felt a sense of joy, which was a great accomplishment. They rejoiced with excitement; because now God dwelled among them, and they had a man of God as their king. They even rejoiced because the land that was promised to their ancestors finally belonged to them.

Have you ever thought about your freedom, the fact that you can come and go whenever you want? My ancestors or the ancestors of many African-Americans had to fight for their freedom just as the Israelites did. They had to fight for the right to work in their gardens, not their masters' or slave owners' cotton fields. They had certain times to be out of bed, to eat, to worship, etc. Like the Israelites, African-Americans were beaten when they failed to follow the rules of their masters. They fought to be treated humanely. God has never left us, and He never will. So, therefore, we will never lose the battle as long as we continue to hold tightly to the safe hand of our Lord.

AmaZING

After the death of King David, who reigned? 1 Chronicles 23:1

I & II Chronicles are the thirteenth and fourteenth books of the Bible, recorded to reunite Israel's people and show King David's linage. The books also encouraged Judah's people to live according to God's laws and contain fascinating information about numerous people: Solomon, Queen Sheba; Asa; and Jehoshaphat. You can even read about Saul's death, King David's reign and death, the reign and death of Solomon, and the spiritual fall of Israel. I have written a summary to introduce you to some of the people mentioned in these books. First, let's talk about Jashobeam, one of the three top leaders under David's command. He killed three-hundred men with the same spear in one battle, 1 Chronicles 11:11. Then there is Eleazar; he was the second-best of David's warriors. He fought with David in a barley pasture against the Philistines in Pasdammim. They beat the Philistines as the other Israelites fled, and he killed a lion in a pit when it was snowing and a 7 ½ foot tall Egyptian.

Jonathan was the commander of David's bodyguards and killed three-hundred soldiers in one battle. He is considered an honorable man because he killed two giants from Moab (1 Chronicles 11:22). And he also fought and killed a giant with twelve toes and twelve fingers in the war at Gath (1 Chronicles 20:6-7). After winning the war against the Edomites, King Amaziah gathered all the idol gods that the people of Seir had and took them home with him. He started bowing and praising them in his kingdom; this made God angry with King Amaziah. So God sent a prophet to ask him, "Why have you sought the gods of the people, which could not rescue their own people from your hand" (1 Chronicles 25:15)? In other words, why did you collect all those idol gods, and why are you worshipping them? King Amaziah was evil to the prophet sent by God, he told him to be quiet. He said I didn't ask you for advice. As the prophet retreated, he said, "I know that God has determined to destroy you, because you have done this and have not heeded my advice, (2 Chronicles 25:15). Even I would like to know why he chose to collect and worship idol gods, things made by man that cannot talk, walk, or even see. He could not believe the prophet, so he kept doing what he was big enough to do. After King Amaziah's death, Judah's people crowned sixteen-year-old Uzziah king. He soon became arrogant and corrupted. So much so, he sinned against God by entering the Temple that was forbidden to everyone except the priest. He burned incense on the altar; approximately eighty-one priests tried to get him to leave the Temple. The fact that they did not want him there made Uzziah mad. As they stood there, leprosy appeared on his forehead; at that point, he was happy to leave. Uzziah remained a leper, the entirety of his life. He lived alone in exile, never entering the Temple again (2 Chronicles 26:21).

AmaZING

> What did Ezra say about his travels during his trip from Babylon to Judea?
>
> Ezra 8:21-23, 31-32

Ezra is the fifteenth book of the Bible. Within Ezra is a census about numerous Jews returning to Judah. They were exiles returning to their homeland or descendant children of the Jews that were ousted. Their job was to finish the Temple. And when it was, the priests dressed in robes and blew trumpets while descendants of Asaph beat cymbals and praised God.

During this period, Cyrus was the king of Persia. God chose him to rebuild the Temple in Jerusalem (Ezra 1:2). So, Ezra sent out letters informing the people of his duties. The hearts of the people in great and low positions was generous; they came bearing gifts, materials, muscles, etc. Ezra donated valuable items that Nebuchadnezzar had stolen from the Temple in Jerusalem. He also donated silver and gold items from his collection.

AmaZING

How did Nehemiah protect himself from danger?

Nehemiah 4:9-23

Nehemiah is the sixteenth book of the Bible. This book records the rebuilding of Jerusalem's walls and the people renewing their faith. One might consider this book to be the autobiography of Nehemiah. Nehemiah was one of the twelve Jewish leaders exiled from Babylon. The king permitted him to return to his home town of Judah to rebuild the city.

Now let's chat about some of the other characters in this book like Carshena, Shethary, Admatha, Tarshish, Merres, Marsena, Menucan, King Xerxes, Esther, and Mordecai. We will start by learning more about King Xerxes first. He ruled over the lands from India to Ethiopia. He resided in a castle in the country of Susa. During his third year as king, he threw a huge party to show off his riches. The party lasted for six months. He sent invitations to all the princes, officials, military officers, noblemen, and provincial officers. He made sure every one of importance was there. After it was over, he threw a party for the moderate to low income people; it lasted only seven days.

At the same time, Queen Vashti had a party for the women in the palace. On the seventh and last day of the party, the king had become intoxicated and instructed his eunuchs to fetch Queen Vashti with only her crown upon her head. She was a very beautiful woman, and he wanted the men to gaze upon her beauty. But Queen Vashti refused to come. That made King Xerxes very angry. He consulted with his seven advisors: Carshena, Shethar, Admatha, Tarshish, Meres, Marsena, and Memucan. After the king, they held the highest positions in his empire. He told them he sent for the queen, but she refused to come, so he asked, what do you think I should do. Memucan said to the king; she embarrassed every man in your empire, and if you don't punish her, that will encourage women everywhere to start disobeying their husbands once they hear about what she did. They advised the king to write a new law and send it to all the Persians and Medes, saying Queen Vashti is banished forever, and another queen would be chosen. The law also stated that this rule could never be changed and implied that this will allow men always to be respected by their wives. King Xerxes did as his advisors said. They added this would ensure that men everywhere would forever rule their homes (Nehemiah 1:21). You can read more to see how the story ends.

AmaZING

> Haman hated the Jews! Why? Esther 3:2, 5-6

Esther is the seventeenth book of the Bible and tells the story of an orphan Jewish girl raised by her cousin, Mordecai (Esther 2:7). It also tells about the Jews in exile and their non-Jewish Persia enemies and how Esther was selected as queen and risked her life to save her people.

After King Xerxes had Queen Vashti banished from his empire, his advisors suggested the king have a beauty pageant within his kingdom. All the beautiful young virgin girls in the kingdom were taken from their homes, dressed in lavished clothing, given beauty treatments, and then taken to Susa, where they were cared for by a eunuch. When the advisors told the king about their scheme, he was pleased, so he instructed them to go ahead with the plan (Esther2:10-6:14). Ester was among the young women taken to Susa for the beauty contest and put under the care of Hegai. He was impressed with her beauty and assigned the best maids to attend to her, gave her a special menu, and placed her in the finest part of the Harem. No one ever asked of her ethnic group or nationality; Mordecai told her uncle never to tell anyone if they did ask. Before the women were taken to the king's bedroom, they had to have six months of oil treatments with myrrh and twelve months of beauty treatments. After a special night with the king, the women were placed in a Harem with his other wives. They were cared for by a eunuch named Shaashgaz, and unless the king asked for one of them, they lived in the palace away from their families and the king.

When Esther was selected to entertain the king, she was instructed by Hegai to be obedient; she did just as she was told. The king loved her more than any of the other women that had visited his chambers. He was so fascinated with Esther that he crowned her queen of his palace. He threw a big banquet to honor Esther as his new queen, and Mordecai was given the privilege to sit at the king's gate (Esther 3:19). One day two of the eunuchs that worked at the palace got mad with King Xerxes and decided he should die. Haman heard them plotting to kill the king, so he told Queen Esther. She went to the king and informed him of their plans. The king checked it out and found it to be true; both eunuchs were hanged.

And then, in chapter three, King Xerxes made Haman, an Agagite, his prime minister. Haman became the second most powerful person in the empire. All the officials had to bow before Haman as a sign of respect, but Mordecai was unwilling to bow to Haman. The officials asked Mordecai time after time why he refused to do as the king commanded, and he would not answer. Finally, they asked Haman how long he would allow Mordecai to disrespect him. That enraged Haman to the point that he decided something must be done. He decided all Jews in the empire should be put to death; because Mordecai was a Jew. To kill all the Jews, Haman came up with a great idea. He thought to himself; I will tell the king there is a race of people under his reign that refuse to obey the laws; because they are from another land. Haman asked the king to write a decree to rid the kingdom of that culture and help with the problem; he would donate 375 tons of silver. King Xerxes gave him the okay by simply giving Haman his signet ring. Haman had all the secretaries of the kingdom write letters to all the officials in every language, informing them that all Jewish people should be killed; no one was to be spared, young or old. The letters were then signed with the king's name and sealed with his ring. Haman told them that for every Jew you kill, you may keep all of their valuables. After the letters were disbursed throughout the kingdom, the people of Susa were confused. They did not understand what they were talking about in the letters.

When Mordecai learned about the letters, he was so upset he ripped off his clothes and put on sackcloth and ashes; then he went to the city crying bitterly. The clothes he put on were clothes of mourning. The Jews throughout the land did as Mordecai did, put on their mourning clothes. Some eunuchs and maids told Queen Esther about Mordecai, and she was saddened. She sent him some clothes, but Mordecai refused to put them on. Then Queen Esther sent for one of King Xerxes' eunuchs, Hathach. She told him to go to Mordecai seeking answers as to what was troubling him. Mordecai told Hathach what Haman had done. He also gave Hathach a copy of the letter to give to Queen Esther. A few days later, Queen Esther put on her royal attire and went to see the king. He saw her coming and welcomed her by holding his gold scepter out (Esther 5:3-7). Well, I don't want to spoil the rest of this wonderful story for you, so I think I will back up like a crab. In other words, I am stopping here so you can look forward to reading all about Esther yourself.

AmaZING

Was Job poor or was he rich?

Job 1:3

Job is the eighteenth book of the Bible and is the first of five wisdom books; it focuses on trials, observation, heart experiences, discernment, folly, and love. The story is about deliverance and the affliction of Job. It describes his suffering, faith, and patience. Job refuted the saying, "if someone is suffering, it is because he/she has sinned." Job was a true believer;

he endured much suffering, both physical and material. But he never lost his faith in God.

One day some bad people were having a meeting, and a man was passing by; he stopped to see what was going on. They told him that they were looking for others to join their group. He asked, who are you, and what is your organization? They said we are the Demons; we do whatever we want to, like disobeying the laws and stealing; and answering only to our leader Natas. We are looking for anyone we can persuade to join in with us. Are you willing to be a part of our group? The man said, no, I fear God, for he is my protector and provider. Because they did not like his answer, they beat and robbed the man of all he had. The next time they saw him, they asked him, are you ready to join us now? The man's answer was still the same no. He said I still fear God, my protector, and my provider (Job 1:6-). Now that you are interested in the story, I will stop here. It is up to you to read on. You will not believe what happened.

AmaZING

What is the longest Psalms? Psalms 119

"Lord, I cry unto thee: make haste unto me; give ear unto my voice, when I cry unto thee." Psalms 141:1

Psalms are the nineteenth book of the Bible. The known Psalms authors include David, Moses, Solomon, and Asaph. All of the other authors are anonymous. This book helps one understand man's relation with God; it contains information on trust, sin, help in times of trouble, and faith or helps one know that God is all-powerful.

If you would like to live a prosperous life or be like a tree living on the banks of a river bearing healthy, delicious fruits each year, you must not take the advice of evil men nor stay in their presence. It is best to stay away from them because evil people are usually unpleasant, ridiculers, even disagreeable people. God sees all we do, and He knows all things (Psalms 1:1-4).

AmaZING

> "For wisdom is better than rubies; and all the things that may be desired are not to be compared to it." Proverbs 8:11

Proverbs is the twentieth book of the Bible. Proverbs seem to be a book of realistic, down-to-earth sayings; or a book of instruction about life, knowledge, and understanding. It contains various subjects such as purity, laziness, controlling the tongue, knowledge, justice, relationships, and wisdom. It will help anyone that desires to live a godly life; because it contains the instructions needed to live a successful life. It also teaches you how to gain wisdom if that is what you want.

Proverbs 1:7-9 states, "The fear of the Lord is the beginning of knowledge: but fools despise wisdom and instruction. My Son, hear the instruction of thy father and forsake not the law of thy mother: For they shall be an ornament of grace unto thy head and chains about thy neck." We can gain wisdom if we follow the instructions given: The first thing we must do is reverence and trust God. We should be ready to learn or be taught, unlike fools, who refuse teachings. We should be prepared and eager to gain knowledge from our parents; because they have become wise from their years of experience. The things you learn from your parents will help you go through life without so much drama or so many errors.

Proverbs is an excellent book for teens, as it tells them that they should search for wisdom instead of money; and that to gain knowledge and understanding is the beginning of godly fear. It will help them deal with a wide range of problems dealing with life, such as instructions on living and sickness, etc.

AmaZING

"And also that every man should eat and drink, and enjoy the good of all his labor, it is the gift of God." Ecclesiastes 3:13

Ecclesiastes is the twenty-first book of the Bible. It is basically about Solomon; it shows life through the things we recognize, like the sun. It not only tells of solar or material things but spiritual things as well. How we enjoy material riches, and it evaluates man.

Ecclesiastes 12:1 states, Remember now thy Creator in the three days of thy youth, while the evil days come not, nor the years draw nigh when thou shalt say, I have no pleasure in them;" Children just because you are young, don't think that you don't need God right now. Do not get caught up in life and the excitement of being young that you do not give God some of your time. You should honor and praise him even now while you are young; don't wait until you are old and can't do the things you once could like: dancing, partying, staying out late, having fun on the beach, etc. God is the Creator of all things, so do not wait until you are too old to enjoy the things you are doing now to give God honor and praise.

AmaZING

I would just like to make a statement about life on this scroll. According to the world it is okay to have sex before marriage; but according to God's word that is incorrect. This is just a notation about the Song of Solomon, from me to you.

Solomon or **The Song of Solomon** is the twenty-second book of the Bible. The theme of the entire book is about love and is also a collection of marriage songs. It seems to be a book of love poems between a man and a woman. And this book tells of the joy of marital love between a man and a woman. It also contains a collection of marriage songs.

It instructs God's people about love, sex, and marriage. It informs the reader that sex is special and that it is something that is shared between a husband and wife, not something that should be taken or done literally. It should be sacred.

Solomon's Song is like the book of Ecclesiastes. Both books explain God's love for the Israelites, God's chosen people, and the love God has for the church, His bride.

AmaZING

"Hear, O havens, and give ear, O earth: for the Lord hath spoken, I have nourished and brought up children, and they have rebelled against me." Isaiah 1:2

Isaiah is the twenty-third book of the Bible. Isaiah's message is twofold: Judah's judgment for her sin; and the restoration and hope for the Israelites, an exiled people.

Well, let's check out a few of the verses in Isaiah. First, we will start with 1:18, "Come now, and let us reason together, saith the Lord: though your sins are as scarlet, they shall be as white as snow; though they are red like crimson, they shall be as wool." Even the sins we commit against God, Himself, He can wash away all of them. God lets us know that no matter how bad our sins are, He will always forgive us for them when we ask with a pure heart. God says that He can take the stain of our sins out of us by cleaning us thoroughly of all our sins, leaving us as white as snow. Even if our sins are crimson or horrible, maybe a sin against God, Himself, He can wash away all or any of them.

I thought this interesting; verse 8:1 contains the longest name that I have ever seen in the Bible or anywhere else. The name is Ma'-her-shal'-al-hash'-baz; God chose this name for a child not yet conceived.

Another interesting fact is about nakedness in the Bible. God instructed Isaiah to take his clothes and sandals off when King Sargon captured the Philistine city. Isaiah obeyed God and did as he was told. He paraded around for approximately three years. "And the Lord said, Like as my servant Isaiah hath walked naked and barefoot three years for a sign and wonder upon Egypt and upon Ethiopia;" Isaiah 20:3. You can read all about Isaiah's nakedness and the Egyptians and Ethiopian prisoners' nakedness within this book.

AmaZING

> Jeremiah compared the worshipping of God to the worshipping of idols. What does he say? Jeremiah 2:13

Jeremiah is the twenty-fourth book of the Bible. He was a great prophet; he lived and prophesied to Judah when times were terrible. He tried to get the people to follow God before the Egyptians defeated them. Jeremiah seems to have had a challenging task because the people had abandoned their faith. He stood by himself for God in the middle of his apostate people.

What do you think is the most deceitful or deceptive thing on Earth, and where is it located? Well, it's the heart, and we all know where the heart is. Jeremiah 17:9 states, "The heart is deceitful above all things, and desperately wicked: who can know it?" There is nothing more deceitful than the heart. It is a wicked trouble organ, yet we need it to live and to love. That should make you wonder how a heart can be so wicked.

AmaZING

> Jerusalem was thrown away like a dirty rag. Why? Lamentations 1:8a

Lamentations or The Lamentations of Jeremiah is the twenty-fifth book of the Bible. Lamenting means to feel deep sorrow or express it by weeping or wailing; mourn; grieve (Webster's Dictionary). This book is a collection of five poems mourning the demolition and destruction of Jerusalem. This book of poems expresses feelings of deep sorrow, weeping, anger, death, and grief.

There was once a city filled with people, but now it is laying waste; because the people have gone away. This city was once fabulous, and the people were plenteous. But now it is deserted, do you want to know why? Indeed, one wants to know what would cause a fabulous city once filled with people to be empty and run down or to be in ruins. Chapters one and two will explain it as you read these grievous poems.

After years of the people being disobedient, the author of Lamentations, Saul (Jeremiah: according to Life Application Study Bible), cried out to God for his people; he said, I cry continually; because I am in so much pain. He said I pour my heart out to you, Lord, for my people. The children are fainting in the streets for lack of food; some look upon their parents' sad faces for help. Others are dying in their mothers' arms.

AmaZING

Why did Ezekiel eat the scroll? And what did he say it tasted like? Ezekiel 3:1-3

Ezekiel is the twenty-sixth book of the Bible; and the 4th of the five prophetic books. Ezekiel was a priest and a prophet. At the age of thirteen, he was taken by the Egyptians with the Jews into slavery. Ezekiel prophesied about the destruction approximately seven years before it happened.

If you have a vivid imagination, think about these things: creatures with four faces and glowing clouds. Chapter one, verse eleven, tells how Ezekiel saw them in June. Ezekiel was looking toward heaven, and he saw a storm brewing in the north. In front of the storm, the clouds were glowing as if with fire, flashing continually. He saw four weird shapes with men's appearance in the center of the fiery clouds, but each one had two wings and four faces. The legs seemed to be human, but their feet were like split hooves or cloven, and they shined as if made of brass. The creatures had hands that looked like human hands, and their wings touched. As Ezekiel continued to observe, he realized that they had three other faces besides a man's face. He noticed on the right side of their heads was a lion's face, on the left side was the face of an ox and finally on the back of their heads were faces of eagles. He also saw two pairs of wings set in the center of their backs and the other pair of wings stretched to connect them. They could only fly forward, never being able to turn.

AmaZING

Four young men were given new names. What were their new names? Daniel 1:7

Daniel or **The Book of Daniel** is the twenty-seventh book of the Bible; and the 5th of five prophetic books. God gave Daniel the knowledge to dreams. There was a king back in biblical times that had an awful dream; it was so bad he could not sleep. Have you ever had a dream like that? The king's name was Nebuchadnezzar. This dream disturbed him so much that he called everyone in his kingdom that he thought could decipher his dream. But no one could, not even his astrologers (2:1-3). You need to read this story; it is fascinating. You will not be able to stop reading until you have read the entire story.

Another great story is about a king that ate grass like a cow or a sick animal. One year after King Nebuchadnezzar had this dream, he walked around on the roof of his palace in Babylon. He believed that he had accomplished everything by himself; he started saying, look at all of this that I have done. He had become boastful and full of pride because he had so much money and territory. He thought I built this dazzling city all by myself. As he spoke, he heard the voice of God; and He said, "...O king

Nebuchadnezzar, to thee, it is spoken; the kingdom departs from thee. And they shall drive thee from men, and thy dwelling shall be with the beasts of the field: they shall make thee eat grass as oxen, and seven times shall pass over thee until thou know that the highest ruleth in the kingdom of men, and giveth it to whomsoever he will. The same hour was the king fulfilled upon Nebuchadnezzar: he was driven from men and did eat grass as oxen, and his body was wet with the dew of heaven, till his hairs were grown like eagles' feathers, and his nails like birds' claws. (Daniel 4:31b-33). God took everything from him and turned him out to pasture as one would do an animal. Within that hour of him speaking, he was ousted from "his" kingdom. He had to live in the wilderness with the animals for seven years, and he ate what the animals ate. Nebuchadnezzar had to stay there until he understood who God is and what man can and cannot do. He had to learn that everything belongs to God; and that God gives what He wants to whomever he pleases. He was in the wilderness for such an extended period that his hair grew very long and looked like the feathers of an eagle. His nails looked like the claws of a bird. Read, learn, and discover more interesting and wonderful scenes within this book.

AmaZING

"Come, and let us return unto the Lord: for he hath torn, and he will heal us; he hath smitten, and he will bind us up." Hosea 6:1

Hosea is the twenty-eighth book of the Bible. Hosea prophesied in Israel under the rule of Jeroboam. His people were disobedient to God's words, and he also carried a heavy burden because of his wife's unfaithfulness.

The people in Hosea's time were disobeying God more and more in each generation. It is the same today; as time goes on, we are getting further away from God and His words. Now the world is a prime example of what Hosea talks about in his book. When I was a child, everyone in the community was like a parent; but people are not like that today. They have changed so much; they can't be trusted with children because of abuse. Parents will tell you, "this is my child; you can't tell them what to do," Statements like that may encourage some children to be rude to their elders. There are still good people in the world; yes, there is some good in everyone, for God is love.

Now let's get back to the story of a disobedient people. These people were making and praising metal gods, images they had made with their hands. So, how can you make a god with your hands? Can it touch you? No, you have to touch it. Can it see you? No, it has no eyes; it has whatever they put on its face. Can it hear you? No, they look like ears; but that is just how they shaped the doll; Can it talk to you? No, it could not speak to them. But in today's society, they make dolls that can talk, among other things. But guess what? They are still unseeing, unhearing, speechless, and human-made items.

AmaZING

What did Joel tell the people of Judah, God wanted them to do?
Joel 2:12

Joel is the twenty-ninth book of the Bible. Joel told his people, Judah's people, that they must repent and that God would bless them spiritually and materially if they would stop sinning.

Joel mentions "the day of the Lord" in 2:1, and he describes it as a dark, gloomy day, with thick and black clouds. He spoke of this day to inform the people of Judah to return to praising and obeying God. They were told God would punish them if they refused. Joel told them they could not escape the punishment of God, even though they may escape other unpleasant situations. For example, we can bounce back from most natural disasters. But when God judges us, His punishment is the final punishment. Joel prophesied a plague of locust that would cover the entire land, devouring all crops. This vision was showing the Judeans the power and might of God during the ultimate judgment.

AmaZING

Amos spoke of two sins that the Israelites were doing. What were they? Amos 2:12

Amos is the thirtieth book of the Bible. This book is about the people of Israel's dishonesty, oppression, and neglect of the words of God. God summoned Amos to go to the northern kingdom of Israel to prophesy.

God gave Amos a vision of three things that would happen to the Israelites if they refused to repent. In his vision, the things he saw were: locust would eat all of their crops; a fire would destroy the land and its inhabitants, and there was a plumb line running along the wall that was going to test their loyalty. As Amos spoke to the Israelites, Amaziah, the priest of Bethel, heard him talking, so Amaziah wrote a note to King Jeroboam stating that Amos was plotting to kill him. "He said you would be killed, and the Israelites will be exiled from Bethel." Then

Amaziah sent a note to Amos saying, go back to Judah and preach, we don't want you here. Read the rest of this beautiful story about Amos and the Israelites to see what happened.

AmaZING

> "For the day of the Lord is near upon all the heathen: as thou has done, it shall be done unto thee: thy reward shall return upon thine own head." Obadiah 1:15

Obadiah is the Thirty-first book of the Bible, the shortest prophetic book. It contains only twenty-one verses. This book is a brutal accusation about the descendants of Esau, the Edomites, who from the very beginning were hostile to Israel. This book is basically about the destruction and disaster of Edom. Near the end of the judgment, the people seem to have started worrying about the Day of the Lord, or the day God's judgment will come upon Edom and other nations.

AmaZING

> The word came to Jonah telling him to do what? Jonah 1:2

Jonah is the thirty-second book of the Bible, and it is the fifth of the twelve books of the Minor Prophets. God instructed Jonah to minister to the Ninevites that he would destroy them; because they were sinful. He was scared, so he went in the opposite direction of Nineveh. We often do that ourselves, God tells us to go right, but we go left. Jonah knew what God wanted him to do, but he thought I am not doing that like most people. Instead of going to the north, he went to the south. He was probably thinking; I will get as far away from here as I can. Running from a situation is not always the best way to solve the problem. Jonah found that out as he found himself in numerous situations, in which one was in the belly of a fish. Jonah had to understand that no matter where he goes, God is there. He is omnipresent. For Jeremiah 23:24 says, "Can anyone hide himself in secret places that I shall not see him? Saith the Lord. Do not I fill Heaven and Earth? Saith the Lord. "And Amos 5:19 "As if a man did flee from a lion, and a bear met him; or went into the house, and leaned his hand on the wall, and a serpent bit him." Once again, it is saying you can't run or hide from God. When we try to run away from what God would have us do, it is like running into a steel wall. Until we do thus saith the Lord, everything we try to do will fail.

AmaZING

Whom did Micah prophesy about? Micah 5:2

Micah is the thirty-third book of the Bile; and the sixth book of the twelve books of the Minor Prophets. Micah's message was similar to Amos' message: the people were committing the same sins as before. He taught the people about God's judgment on sin; he also told the people that deliverance would come through Jesus, the Messiah.

This book also tells how the poor people of Samaria and Judah were misused. The rich were getting richer, while the poor people had less and less to survive. The upper class was abusing the women and children as well. The rich lived lavish lives, unlike the people they continually oppressed. Chapter 6:8 says, "He hath showed thee, O man, what is good; and what doth the Lord require of thee, but to do justly, and to love mercy, and to walk humbly with thy God?" In other words, God had shown us what is right according to His laws; and that we should be humble and have mercy. For He has told and shown us how we should live, love one another, help each other and treat everyone as if they were your family.

AmaZING

What was Nahum's nationality? Nahum 1:1

Nahum is the thirty-fourth book of the Bible; and the seventh of the twelve books of the Minor Prophets. He predicted the collapse of Nineveh, Assyria's capital city. Very little information if given on Nahum, except that he lived in Elkosh and that God gave him a vision concerning Nineveh. In his dream or vision, Nahum was told to go to Nineveh to tell the people that God was angry because they had become corrupt, 1:1-2. They were so evil that God was going to destroy Nineveh if they refused to repent.

The book of Nahum is also about a vision given for the good of the people. He was to warn the Ninevehites about their arrogance, oppression, and idol worship.

AmaZING

What did Habakkuk say would happen? Habakkuk 1:6

Habakkuk is the thirty-fifth book of the Bible; and the eighth of the twelve books of the Minor Prophets. He was a prophet to whom God gave a vision to answer questions that concerned him. In the first question, he asked God, "O Lord, how long shall I cry, and thou wilt not hear! Even cry out unto thee of violence, and thou wilt not save!" (2:2). He wants to know how long he has to pray to God for help. Habakkuk says I pray, and I pray, but you don't seem to hear me. There is so much violence going on; why don't you help me? Then one day, God answered him. He said, "Behold ye among the heathen, and regard, and wonder marvelously: for I will work a work in your days, which ye will not believe, though it be told you. For, lo, I raise up the Chaldeans, that bitter and hasty nation, which shall march through the breadth of the land, to possess the dwelling places that are not theirs. They are terrible and dreadful: their judgment and their dignity shall proceed of themselves" (1:5-7). Sometimes instead of reacting, we need to sit back and let nature take its course. Look around you and be amazed at what God can do. As you look at the birds, bees, and even the trees, you will truly be amazed. God can, and He sometimes does use our enemies to fight our battles. We have to be willing and trusting enough to give our issues to God. At that point, we can sit back and watch Him do what He said He would do.

Now let's talk about the second question. "Art thou not from everlasting, O Lord my God, mine Holy One? We shall not die. O Lord, thou hast ordained them for judgment; and, O mighty God, thou has established them for correction" (1:12). I have interpreted this verse to say, O Lord God, the Most Holy One, You will always be. But are you planning to wipe out the human race? God, I hope not. How can you allow the Babylonians, a cruel and unjust people, to correct or punish us for our sins? For they have committed far worst sins than we have. Habakkuk did just as we do today. He asked God a question and did not like the answer he gave. We are not always going to get the answer(s) we want, and a lot of times, we have to learn to live with the solution(s) God gives us. Habakkuk realized that God's focus was not on his enemies, but instead, it was on Habakkuk and his people. We are dealing with times like that now; people kill each other for just because reasons. We take no interest in love or helping anyone except ourselves.

Habakkuk and Jonah are somewhat alike; in that, both prophets were aggravated with the positions in which they found themselves placed. The only difference is Jonah tried to run away from God, but Habakkuk decided to pray to God about his situation.

AmaZING

"Hold thy peace at the presence of the Lord God: for the day of the Lord is at hand: for the Lord hath prepared a sacrifice, he hath bid his guests." Zephaniah 1:7

Zephaniah is the thirty-sixth book of the Bible; and the ninth of the books of the Minor Prophets. He saw God's horrible judgment on some of the nations, so he urged the people to stop sinning. He tried to assure them that God would dwell with them if they would reform from sin and follow Him. Zephaniah prayed for the people of Lebanon always; because they were wicked, sinful, and deceitful people. "Woe to her that is filthy and polluted, to the oppressing city!" (3:1). Chapter three is a prayer that he chanted for the people.

During the second year of the reign of King Darius, God sent Zephaniah to give the people a message: "I will consume man and beast; I will consume the fowls of the heaven, and the fishes of the sea, and the stumblingblocks with the wicked; and I will cut off man from off the land, saith the Lord" (1:3). Zephaniah said that they should not fall into the same trap that their ancestors fell into; he even encouraged them to repent from their sinful ways. Then God sent another message to them by Zephaniah two years later. So read on to learn what God did and how the people reacted to the pleas of God.

AmaZING

According to Haggai, Christ was referred to as what? Haggai 2:6-7

Haggai is the thirty-seventh book of the Bible; and the tenth book of the twelve books of the Minor Prophets. He encouraged the people to stop building houses for themselves and help finish rebuilding the Temple, which they had delayed for approximately two decades.

They were after riches and lavish living. They had no time to work on the Temple. Haggai reminded the Jews that they were supposed to be rebuilding the Temple.

AmaZING

"Then said I, O my lord, what are these? And the angel that talked with me said unto me, I will shew thee what these be." Zechariah 1:9

Zechariah is the thirty-eighth book of the Bible; and the eleventh book of the twelve books of Minor Prophets. Zechariah and Haggai prophesied near the same period, but Zechariah was younger than Haggai.

He was one of the seven priests appointed to play his trumpet at the wall's rededication after returning from Babylon.

AmaZING

In Malachi chapter one, he posted several evils or sins, what are they? Malachi 1

Malachi is the thirty-ninth book of the Bible; and the twelfth of the twelve books of Minor Prophets. Malachi's book tells of how the priests neglected their duty. He also informs one of how the people worshiped idols and ignored God. Malachi is the last book of the Old Testament.

After returning to their homeland, building fine homes, and reinforcing the wall around the city to keep their enemies out and their city safe, they forgot about God and started doing sinful things. They praised God, but that was just for show; it wasn't from their hearts. Malachi told them that God would punish them unless they returned to Him. But do you think they listened to Malachi? As you read the book of Malachi, you will find out.

NEW TESTAMENT

AmaZING

> Which books are considered the four gospels? Matthew, Mark, Luke and John

Matthew or **The Gospel According to St. Matthew** is the first book in the N.T., the fourth book in the Bible, and the first four Gospels. This book aims to convince the Jewish people that Jesus is the Messiah and a descendant of David.

As believers in Christ, we should not worry about food, clothes, or water; because God gave us life, just like he did the birds of the air. He takes care of us, so surely He will do the same for us, His children. Matthew 6:31 states, "Therefore take no thought, saying What shall we eat? or, What shall we drink? or, Wherewithal shall we be clothed?" People worry about the wrong things in life, I suppose because we know that we work to provide for ourselves; and that parents provide food and shelter for their children. However, God supplies our clothes even if we have to go to the Salvation Army to get them. He knows what we need, and we should not worry about these things. If we put Him first, He takes care of all of our needs.

The book of Matthew lets us know that we should love ye one another, even our foes. We should treat people the way we would want them to treat us. Even if a person has mistreated you or is mistreating you, don't be evil to them. I am not saying stay in an abusive relationship (mental or physical); no one wants to be or should be abused. Love everyone, even if you have to do it from a distance. Don't hold a grudge, and learn how to forgive. You may never forget when someone mistreats you, but that is okay. Psalms 37:1 says, "Fret not thyself because of evildoers, neither be thou envious against the workers of iniquity." Trust in God and always be the best that you can be. Surely we all will experience unpleasant things, but that will help you grow spiritually in Christ. Don't worry about evil or wicked people, and never envy people that treat you wrong.

AmaZING

> "This is my blood of the new testament, which is shed for many."
> St. Mark 14:24b

Mark or **The Gospel According to St. Mark,** is the second book in the N.T., the forty-first book in the Bible, and the second of the four Gospels. He tells about baptism and the ascension of Jesus Christ. In this book, he focuses on the miracles and the works of Jesus. It also contains at least twenty miracles performed by Jesus.

Should children meet Jesus? The answer is yes; after reading Mark 10:14b-15, those verses tell how Jesus felt about little children. Some parents brought their children to see Jesus, when they arrived, the disciples were turning them away. They believed it would waste the precious time of Jesus for children to be there. Jesus saw what they were doing and told the disciples to leave them alone, let them come to me. He said to them that God's kingdom belongs to people with the heart of a child. Anyone who wants to be a part of God's kingdom must be humble and faithful like a child. And it states, "Suffer the little children to come unto me and forbid them not: for of such is the kingdom of God. Verily I say unto you; whosoever shall not receive the kingdom of God as a little child, he shall not enter therein."

Luke or **The Gospel According To St. Luke,** is the third book in the N.T., the forty-second book in the Bible, and the third of the four Gospels. Luke was a physician and the companion to Paul, the Apostle. Luke seems to be the only Gospel that mentions the childhood of our Lord, Jesus Christ. Luke traveled with Paul on numerous occasions, teaching the Gospel.

Who can and will the Devil, Satan try to tempt? He tried to tempt Jesus, the Son of God. If you don't believe me read Luke 4:1-13. Now that you know he tried to tempt Jesus, you should know that he will try to tempt you too. Matthew 26:41 says, "Watch and pray, that ye enter not into temptation: the spirit indeed is willing, but the flesh is weak." Always be on your best behavior, praying continually. That is the only way to keep the Devil off your back. The Spirit is God within us, and it is always struggling with the flesh.

James 1:13 says, "Let no man say when he is tempted, I am tempted of God: for God cannot be tempted with evil, neither tempteth he any man:" Keep that in mind, when you desire to do wrong; that it is not God's doing. Because God is love, and He never tempts anyone to do bad things.

John or **The Gospel According To St. John** is the fourth book in the N.T., the forty-third book in the Bible, and the fourth of the four Gospels. John recorded the beginning of Jesus' ministry and his teachings to the apostles during the Last Supper.

How long do you believe Jesus has been in the world? Well, John 1:1 states, "In the beginning was the Word, and the Word was with God, and the Word was God." God's Word has always been and will always be with us. Likewise, Jesus Christ, our Savior, shall always be with us, for He is the Son of God the Father.

Just what is the living water? The living water, according to John 4:10b is, "…If thou knewest the gift of God, and who it is that saith to thee, Give me to drink; thou wouldest have asked of him, and he would have given thee living water." It is water that calms your fears and puts one closer to God. The closer you get to God, the more you want. It's like having a best friend; the closer you become, the more time you spend together.

AmaZING

> What did Ananias and his wife, Sapphira do to the Holy Spirit?
>
> Acts 5:1-11

Acts or **The Acts of the Apostles** is the forty-fourth book of the Bible. The book of Acts is full of the early history of the Apostolic Church. It begins with Jesus' ascension to heaven. It follows the growth of Rome, Greece, Asia Minor, and Syria as Christianity spreads through those areas.

Do you know where Jesus lives? First of all, he should live in your heart. The kingdom where he lives is in Heaven with

God the Father. Acts 1:11b says, "Ye men of Galilee why stand ye gazing up into heaven? This same Jesus, which is taken up from you into heaven, shall so come in like manner as ye have seen him go into heaven." Jesus has ascended to heaven, and someday He will return.

Now let's talk about Africans or people of color in the Bible. Do you know where to look? Maybe not, so I have listed some of the locations for you to read: Acts 8:27; Genesis 9:15, 10:1-32, 25:25; Daniel 10:6; Psalms 68:31 and Jeremiah 13:23. Anytime you see Ethiopian(s) in the Bible, this refers to African, black, or people of color. Now you can read and research on your own, learning about African heritage as you go.

I have learned a tip for you while doing my research; God will let you know where he wants you to go and what he wants you to do. All you have to do is listen, be humble, and have an open heart. If you don't believe it, read Acts 16:6-10.

AmaZING

> "For whether we live, we live unto the Lord; and whether we die, we die unto the Lord: whether we live therefore, or die, we are the Lord's." Romans 14:8

Romans or **The Epistle of Paul The Apostle To The Romans** is the forty-fifth book of the Bible. The writer of Romans', Paul, professes himself to be a slave for our Lord and Savior Jesus Christ. He wrote the book to tell the church the good news about Jesus and encourage them to stay strong and continue their faith.

In Romans chapter 1:2-3, he proceeds to write the good news, "(Which he had promised afore by his prophets in the holy scriptures,) concerning his Son Jesus Christ our Lord, which was made of the seed of David according to the flesh." He reminds the Romans that God's good news was told long ago by prophets in the Old Testament. The good news was about God's only Son, Jesus Christ. He was born into the world like a human through the royal family of King David. After his death, he was raised by the Holy Spirit to prove that He was the Son of God. People need to be encouraged to believe and obey God's words, the good news. And they should tell people about Jesus, and they need to believe what they are teaching.

Have you ever heard of intercessory prayer? Well, Romans 1:9 says, "For God is my witness, whom I serve with my spirit in the gospel of his Son, that without ceasing I make mention of you always in my prayers;" This type of prayer that Paul prayed for the church is called intercessory prayer. We intercede when we pray for someone other than ourselves. It could be someone in your home, church, circle, someone that has never prayed or does not know how to pray, etc. We should always pray for our political leaders, church leaders, anyone in a leadership position; that they stay strong in Christ so that they have the right motives. I have listed some scriptures here about prayer; maybe you will feel the need to pray for others as you read them: 1 Timothy 2:1; Matthew 18:19-20, 21:22; Ephesians 6:10-18; John 16:23-24, 17:1-26 and the book of Habakkuk is an intercessory prayer.

Now let's talk about sin. How did sin enter the world? "Wherefore, as by one man sin entered into the world, and death by sin; and so death passed upon all men, for that all have sinned:" (5:12). The man spoken about in this verse is named Adam. You can read about his sin in the book of Genesis. He caused sin and death to enter the world. It was at that moment all people started growing old, even dying. Now whom do you think promotes sin? First Peter 5:8 says, "Be sober, be vigilant; because your adversary the devil, as a roaring lion, walketh about, seeking whom he may devour." This means we should be careful at all times, because Satan, the Devil, is continually trying to encourage God's people to do wrong. Satan watches and tries to catch us when we are down, maybe in sickness, in grief, or joblessness. We must pray and pray to stay out of the way of sin.

AmaZING

> "But I would have you know, that the head of every man is Christ; and the head of the woman is the man; and the head of Christ is God." 1 Corinthians 11:3

I Corinthians & II Corinthians or The First Epistle Of Paul The Apostle To The Corinthians is the forty-sixth book of the Bible. Paul wrote these books to inform the people about their problems within the church and offer them solutions. He wanted the people to live Christian lives in a godless sinful nation." Paul, called to be an apostle of Jesus Christ through the will of God, and Sosthenes our brother" (1 Corinthians 1:1). Paul also wrote to tell the teachers to stop giving false information to the people. He instructed the people to stop bickering among themselves and have peace in the church to give God the praise he deserves.

Who did Paul send to help the church with their problems? "For this cause have I sent unto you Timotheus, who is my beloved son, and faithful in the Lord, who shall bring you into remembrance of my ways which be in Christ, as I teach everywhere in every church" (1Corinthians 4:17). Earlier in the chapter, Paul talks about how he wanted the people to be ashamed of their sinful ways and to warn them at the same time. So Timotheus taught the church the truth about Christ.

AmaZING

"Now a mediator is not a MEDIATOR of one, by God is one." Galatians 3:20 (God doesn't need anyone to convey a message; but man definitely needs something or somebody.)

Galatians or **The Epistle Of Paul The Apostle To The Galatians** is the forty-eighth book of the Bible. The book is a letter from Paul to the Christians in Galatia, and it encourages the Galatians to keep their faith and believe they will be free.

Within the book of Galatians, you can find something called the fruit of the spirit. So let's talk about fruits, something we all love, right? There are so many types of fruits in the world. What is your favorite? My favorite is the fruit of the spirit; they are located in Galatians 5:22-23. And it reads, "But the fruit of the spirit is love, joy, peace, longsuffering, gentleness, goodness, faith, Meekness, temperance: against such, there is no law." When we allow the Holy Spirit to influence or govern our lives, we will develop all of those fruits: joy, to experience happiness; love, a feeling a parent should have for their baby or a fondness for a particular food, etc.; peace, no fighting or bickering, longsuffering, learning how to be patient; gentleness, being kind or showing kindness; goodness, being good or polite; faith, believing in yourself and whole heartily in God; meekness, patience or modesty and temperance, having self-control. I tried to explain what each word means to me; each word has other meanings, also.

AmaZING

> "And be ye kind one to another, tenderhearted, forgiving one another, even as God for Christ's sake hath forgiven you."
> Ephesians 4:32

Ephesians or **The Epistle Of Paul The Apostle To The Ephesians** is the forty-ninth book of the Bible. This letter was written by Paul when he was imprisoned; in it, he told the Christians that they should praise God because He continually blessed them spiritually, through Christ Jesus. He encouraged the Christians to be strong in their faith. He said, "Blessed be the God and Father of our Lord Jesus Christ, who hath blessed us with all spiritual blessings in heavenly places in Christ:" Ephesians 1:3.

I want to talk about Ephesians 2:5-6, "Even when we are dead in sins, hath quickened us together with Christ, (by grace ye are saved;) and hath raised us together, and made us sit together in heavenly places in Christ Jesus:" We were spiritually dead and cursed because of our sins or sinful nature, but God is so compassionate and loving that he gave us a second chance when God raised Jesus from the grave. No, we didn't deserve it; but because He loves us so much, He sent His Son, Jesus, to live here on Earth and then die at the hands of man. But now He is back in Heaven with God, the Father.

AmaZING

> "Grace be unto you, and peace, from God our Father, and from the Lord Jesus Christ. I thank my God upon every remembrance of you," Philippians 1:2-3

Philippians or **The Epistle of Paul The Apostle To The Philippians** is the fiftieth book of the Bible. This book is a letter of joy written by Paul to express his appreciation to the Philippians because of the love and faith they showed toward the church.

Everyone needs to know how to have good clean thoughts; Philippians 4:8 tells us how to train our minds to think clearly. "Finally, brethren, whatsoever things are true, whatsoever things are honest, whatsoever things are just, whatsoever things are pure, whatsoever things are lovely, whatsoever things are of good report; if there be any virtue and if there be any praise, think on these things." When we sit around with idle minds, we should think about one of the things listed in the above verse. We should fix our minds on true, honorable, and righteous thoughts. We should think about God, and how wonderful He is, and what we can do to offer up genuine praise to Him.

AmaZING

> "Let the word of Christ dwell in you richly in all wisdom; teaching and admonishing one another in psalms and hymns and spiritual songs, singing with grace in your hearts to the Lord." Colossians 3:16

Colossians or **The Epistle of Paul The Apostle To The Colossians** is the fifty-first book of the Bible. Colossians is a short letter written by Paul demanding the Christians to keep their faith in God. Paul wanted the Christians to know what they were doing that was ungodly. He told them Jesus Christ would meet their needs if they believed in Him.

If you have or had a job and did not like it, what would you do? According to Colossians 3:22-23, you should take pride in it. No matter what type of work you do, you should do your best at it, and you should also be obedient to those over you or above you. You should do your job as if it is the job you desire, not just when you are under supervision, but you should do your very best at all times. Be happy to have a job and work hard as if you are working to please God, not man because all of our rewards come from God.

AmaZING

> "For God hath not appointed us to wrath, but to obtain salvation by our Lord Jesus Christ." 1 Thessalonians 5:9

I & II Thessalonians or **The First Epistle Of Paul The Apostle To The Thessalonians** are books fifty-two and fifty-three of the Bible. Paul wrote these letters to encourage Timothy; and tell him exactly what he should be doing, in the name of Jesus.

To live a Christian life, we must do three essential things without fail. Do you know what they are or how to find them in the Bible? Let me help you, look in 1 Thessalonians 5:16-18 for the answer. "Rejoice evermore. Pray without ceasing. In everything give thanks: for this is the will of God in Christ Jesus concerning you." You should always do your best to be cheerful; you should pray regularly, even when things are not going the way you think they should; and finally, in the name of our Lord and Savior Jesus Christ, give thanks for everything. Please do not take anything for granted; this is what God wants us to do.

In 2 Thessalonians 3:1-5, Paul, a true prophet of God, asked for prayer for the prophets working with him and for himself. Then he asked the Christians to pray that God's words spread throughout the world; he asked the church to pray for protection for them as they traveled from place to place, teaching God's word. He also asked for protection from humankind's dangers, sickness, and any other struggles they may face. Now that is what we as Christians should do daily; we have to pray for our teachers, preachers, pastors, evangelist, presidents, governors, etc., and ourselves. Pray that as you learn the words of God, that you receive it and live it in the name of our Lord Jesus Christ.

AmaZING

"Let no man despise thy youth: but be thou an example of the believers, in word, in conversation, in charity, in spirit, in faith, in purity." 1 Timothy 4:12

I & II Timothy or **The First Epistle Of Paul The Apostle To Timothy** are the fifty-fourth and fifty-fifth books of the Bible. Paul wrote these books or letters to encourage Timothy to keep doing what he knew was right and make sure he knew what he was supposed to be doing in his teachings to the Christians. Timothy was to be an example for the believers in love, faith, etc.

Some people have often asked, or out of fear of asking, they have wondered, are all prophets, preachers, teachers, etc., sent from God? The answer to the question is no. Let's look at 1 Timothy 4:1-2, "Now the Spirit speaketh expressly, that in the latter times some shall depart from the faith, giving heed to seducing spirits, and doctrines of devils; speaking lies in hypocrisy; having their conscience seared with a hot iron;" To me, these verses say that as time goes on the Holy Spirit has told us that many believers in the church will turn away from the living word. They will change the word to suit whatever situation they want you to believe. Once they change the word, it becomes a lie, making them liars. They pretend to be men or women of God, but their works are dead; they have become Satan workers. They will become so complacent with their lies that their conscience does not work anymore. They will become dead in Christ. How can you know a false teacher from a man of God? You need to read Matthew 7:15, 15:6-9, 24:4-5, 24; Corinthians 2:7, 11:3-13, and Romans 16:18; these verses will help you understand or distinguish between true and false prophets. Many other verses can also help you; I have listed a few of them.

Do you want to know why God gave His word in writing? 2 Timothy 2:16 says, "All scripture is written by inspiration of God, and is profitable for doctrine, for reproof, for correction, for instruction in righteousness: That the man o God may be perfect, thoroughly furnished unto all good works." So, God gave His word to us to inform us; and the reason for the Bible is to inspire us and teach us how to live godly lives. God's word instructs us on how to live Holy. It is a map that is printed and easy to follow, leading to heaven's pearly gates. A map that also leads us to a God that loves us so much that He sent Jesus Christ, His only Son, here to live among us as an example of Holy living. If you read John 3:16-17, you will become more knowledgeable about Jesus Christ and why He came to live among us.

AmaZING

Place your own notes or verse on this scroll, from the book of Titus.

_____

_____

_____

_____

Titus or **The Epistle Of Paul To Titus** is the fifty-sixth book of the Bible. Paul wrote this book or letter to a young minister named Titus to encourage him and explain some of the problems he may have to face during his ministry. He was a new convert in Christ. Paul sent him to Crete as a leader to supervise the Christians there. It was so bad that Paul sent him a letter encouraging him to continue in leadership and encourage him to stay pure in a sinful community.

Within this book, find out if you can become defiled; and if so, how? If your heart is pure, all the things around you are righteous and clean. But if it is evil in your heart, it surrounds you, so the only thing within our space or heart is evil. It can affect your mind, your ways, and according to Titus 1:15, even your conscience can become defiled or dirty. And we all know that anything dirty or defiled is not worth having.

Where was Paul when he wrote the book or letter of Philemon?
Philemon 1:1

Philemon or **The Epistle Of Paul To Philemon** is the fifty-seventh book of the Bible. Philemon is the shortest book or letter written by Paul; He encouraged Philemon to take his runaway slave, Onesimus, back as a Christian. Paul seems to have been concerned about Onesimus. And he wanted to know how Philemon would react to his request as a brotherhood in Christ. Onesimus stole some money from his master, Philemon, and ran away, but he returned to Philemon because of Paul.

AmaZING

> "Let us therefore come boldly unto the throne of grace, that we may obtain mercy, and find grace to help in time of need."
> Hebrews 4:16

Hebrews or **The Epistle Of Paul The Apostle Of The Hebrews** is the fifty-eighth book of the Bible. Hebrews was written to encourage the Jewish Christians to put their faith in Jesus Christ; because Jesus is all they needed if they believed. The eleventh chapter of Hebrews focuses on faith. "Now faith is the substance of things hoped for, the evidence of things not seen" 11:1. We are asked to have faith in a God we have never seen, but if you believe in Him with your whole heart, you can feel His presence.

When you meet a stranger, should you chat or even feed them if they ask for food? It is stated in Hebrews 13:2, "Be not forgetful to entertain strangers; for thereby some have entertained angels unawares." We should be careful when we ignore people that ask for help, but at the same time, we have to pray. By that, I mean people will lie, steal, and even kidnap you if you are not careful, so continue to pray, and if you need to help someone, God will show you. Often, we need to slow down long enough to listen or be in the presence of God.

AmaZING

> "Let no man say when he is tempted, I am tempted of God: for God cannot be tempted with evil, neither tempteth he any man: But every man is tempted, when he is drawn away of his own lust and enticed." James 1:13-14

James or **The General Epistle of James** is the fifty-ninth book of the Bible. James wrote this book and introduced himself in James 1:1a. "James, a servant of God and the Lord Jesus Christ,..." Written to the twelve tribes which were scattered abroad, he insisted that words were not examples of a good disciple, but a good example was working.

Did you believe God tempts us before you read the verses above? Now you know that he does not. Satan, the Devil tempts us. Now that you know who tempts us to do evil or have evil thoughts, I will give you some references to read all about it for yourself. Let's start with Hebrew 4:15, Matthew 26:41, Luke 22:46, and James 1:2-4. So who is the tempter? The tempter is Satan. I have listed the following verses to allow you to research: 1 Corinthians 10:13; 11 Corinthians 11:15; 1 John 2:15-17 and 1 Timothy 6:9.

AmaZING

"Grace and peace be multiplied unto you through the knowledge of God, and of Jesus our Lord." 2 Peter 1:2

I & II Peter or **The First Epistle General Of Peter** are the sixty and sixty-first books or letters of the Bible. Peter is one of the apostles of Jesus. He was a fisherman before he left his boat to follow Him. The letters were written to encourage believers to trust and have faith in the Lord continually.

Would you like to know why we experience trials and temptations? It is because our faith is tested as we go through different situations or problems. It shows God just how strong or determined we are. For example, if you lost your job, you should look to God, not drugs. Often, God allows us to go through trials before he places us where he wants us to be. It is important to God that our faith is strong, not wavering, and not even a little. You may have heard someone use the words <u>unwavering faith</u> while trying to encourage someone. It is essential to God that we believe in Him entirely, and it should be important to us, for, with God, all things are possible.

We all speak of love from time to time, but just what is love? And whom shall we love? God is love. He sent his Son into this sinful world to save the souls of you and me. You can read about that in John 3:16-16. There are so many verses about love in the Bible; I will quote two of them now: "...That we love one another. And this is love that we walk after his commandments. This is the commandment, That, as ye have heard from the beginning, ye should walk in it." 2 John 1:5b-6. If we truly love God, we as Christians should follow His commandments. In these letters, you will learn much about love; because he wrote to the church about love. You can find an emphasis on love in other books of the Bible. Some are: First Corinthians 13:4-5, 8, 8:1 & 14:1; Acts 20:28; Matthew 5:44; Jude 1:21, etc.

AmaZING

> Whosoever believeth that Jesus is the Christ is born of God: and every one that loveth him that begat loveth him also that is begotten of him." 1 John 5:1

I, II, & III John or **The First Epistle General Of John** are the sixty-second, sixty-third, and sixty-fourth books or letters of the Bible. Sin is the main focus in his letters; we are instructed to stay away from sin. When we sin, we should pray in the name of Jesus Christ and ask for forgiveness. "My little children, these things I write unto you, that ye sin not. And if any man sin, we have an advocate with the Father, Jesus Christ the righteous:" First John 2:1. These books are short, but John makes his point.

In First John chapter three, he writes about God's incredible love and how much He loves us. He also answers the question that people often wonder about; how can I tell if I am a child of God's or a follower of Satan. First John 3:10-11 says, "In this the children of God are manifest, and the children of the Devil: whosoever doeth not righteousness is not of God, neither he that loveth not his brother. For this is the message that ye heard from the beginning, that we should love one another." After reading these verses, you should know who you are following, God or the Devil, Satan.

AmaZING

> "To the only wise God our Savior, be glory and majesty, dominion and power, both now and ever. Amen." Jude 1:25

Jude or **The General Epistle of Jude** is the sixty-fifth book of the Bible. Jude wrote this letter to warn and encourage the disciples to teach the Bible just as written, word-for-word, for the Bible has not changed. And to tell them to be aware of the false teachers among them, teaching false doctrine. He said they tell the people after they become Christians that they can do anything and not be punished. "Beloved, when I gave all diligence to write unto you of the common salvation, it was needful for me to write unto you and exhort you that ye should earnestly contend for the faith which was once delivered unto the saints. For there are certain men crept in unawares, who were before of old ordained to this condemnation, ungodly men, turning the grace of our God into lasciviousness, and denying the only Lord God, and our Lord Jesus Christ" Jude 1:3-4. In the verses above, Jude was trying to warn the Christians about the false teachers who were trying to get them to turn away from their faith. He instructed the Christians to be watchful and alert when a false teacher approaches them. Jude told the Christians to stay focused on Christ and remember all things God had done for them. In my words (Even in today's society, Christians must be ready because false teachers are still here today).

AmaZING

> "And if any man shall take away from the words of the book of this prophecy, God shall take away his part out of the book of life, and out of the holy city, and from the things which are written in this book." Revelation 22:19

Revelation or **The Revelation Of Saint John The Divine** is the sixty-sixth book of the Bible. Revelation contains many mysterious images of as if you are reading a science fiction and mystery novel written together. I encourage you to read this book, it is inspiring, and it gives us hope; in the end, Jesus, our Lord, and Savior comes to take us home. If you have a vivid imagination, you should picture some of the images in your mind.

In Revelation 1:1, John dreamed of things that would happen in the future and about Jesus Christ. God sent one of His angels to explain John's vision, and he recorded everything he heard and everything he saw about God and Jesus Christ.

Printed in the United States
by Baker & Taylor Publisher Services